Social Media Marketing:

Mastering The Power Of Online Networking

Daniel Powers

EBK Books
Paramount, CA

Library of Congress Cataloging-in-Publication
Social Media Marketing: Mastering The
Power of Online Networking
by Daniel Powers
ISBN: 978-1-936828-31-9

First Edition January 2015

Contents

58 Social Media Tips for Content Marketing

Content marketing and social media make a great team. Think Laurel and Hardy. Woodward and Bernstein. Jordan and Pippen.

No content marketing strategy is complete without a strong social media strategy. As Jay Baer says, social media is the fuel to set your content on fire.

According to 2013 research from CMI and MarketingProfs, B2B marketers use an average of five social media channels to distribute content, whereas B2C marketers use four. Whether you're just getting started with social media or looking to fine-tune your plan, this guide is for you.

This section includes a collection of best practices for the top social media channels that content marketers use to reach their audiences, including examples of brands that have found social media success. Over the course of this book, we'll cover:

▶ Social networks like Facebook, Twitter, Google+, and LinkedIn

► Video channels like YouTube and Vimeo

► Photo sharing sites like Instagram and Flickr

► Online communities like Pinterest, Foursquare, and Quora

► Niche content sharing sites like Tumblr, StumbleUpon, and SlideShare

First, let's take a look at the social networks we all hold near and dear.

Facebook

You need more than just an interesting subject.

Even if your product category is naturally interesting, execution is very important. Spend time posting well-edited photos and well-written copy. Volume certainly isn't everything on Facebook; consistent quality is much more significant.

It's good to be brief, but it's better to be good.

Short messages stand out on Facebook — but long messages work if they're compelling.

Communicate your message succinctly unless you absolutely need the extra words.

Use smarter targeting.

Page Post Targeting (PPT) is a new service from Facebook that allows you to handpick your audience, allowing you to deliver a clear message to a smaller group. For instance, you can direct your message to reach women between the ages of 25-35 who have "liked" your page. (Learn how to use PPT at http://contentmarketinginstitute.com/2012/09/how-to-use-facebooks-newest-feature-to-deliver-targeted-content/)

Measure fan engagement.

Finding your Facebook impact means measuring how fans interact with your content. That way, you can figure out which messages inspire action — and create more like them.

(Here are five engagement benchmarks: http://contentmarketinginstitute.com/2011/01/faceboo k-engagement/)

Who uses Facebook well?

Pet brand PurinaOne represents Facebook marketing that uses phenomenal storytelling to stand out.

▶ Longer posts, supplemented with a picture, tell compelling stories.

▶ Posts are well written and inspire hundreds of comments from fans.

▶ Each piece of content is highly relevant to the brand's audience.

Twitter

Tell a story through your tweets.

Present a consistent voice to tell the story of your industry and your brand. Each post should be compelling in its own right, but an inconsistent tone confuses the audience. (Learn how to make your social media voice consistent: http://contentmarketinginstitute.com/2012/05/how-to-maintain-a-consistent-social-persona/)

Make use of hashtags.

Including 1-3 relevant hashtags with your tweet makes it simple for people to find your content. Creating an original hashtag and linking it to a specific campaign is an even better use of the tactic.

Use it as a testing ground.

Tweet your original content, and keep tabs on which pieces of content get more shares. Use this information to direct your future content efforts.

Cover industry events.

To offer insights in real time, live tweet coverage of events that are significant for your audience. That way, your brand can act as the eyes and ears for individuals who can't make it to the event.

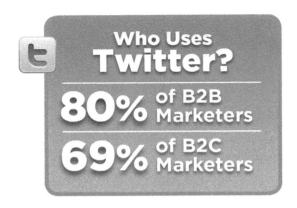

Who uses Twitter well?

With 270,000+ followers, food chain Taco Bell has found a great social media niche for its nationwide brand.

▶ Even followers with small influence get retweets and responses. The brand's voice is down-to-earth and (at times) hilarious.

▶ Events and promotions get great visibility.

▶ Hashtags, especially trending topics, ensure even non-followers can find the brand's tweets.

YouTube and Vimeo

Enable video embedding.

Make sure embedding is enabled, allowing other users to post your videos to their websites.

Mix professional and homegrown videos.

Just because you don't always have a professional videographer at your disposal doesn't mean you can't make great videos. Showcase professional videos alongside homegrown ones to help humanize your brand.

Show, don't tell.

Demonstrating your products or services in action is a much more effective way to create compelling videos than talking about what you do.

Keep it short.

Your audience's attention span can be measured in seconds, even for video content. Keep your content short — less than a minute long, if possible — to deliver a succinct message.

Think compilations, not long shots.

If you do create long-form video, give your audience little snippets of content that piece together a coherent narrative. Developing a video with a single shot (like a speaker presenting for five minutes) can easily fatigue your audience. (Take a look at some video tips and examples: http://contentmarketinginstitute.com/2012/10/create-video-content-that-actuallreally-works/)

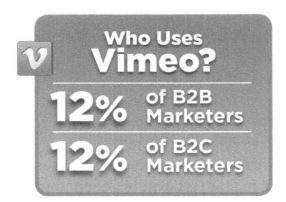

Who uses YouTube and Vimeo well?

Major insurance brand Allstate maintains a fully branded YouTube channel that capitalizes on the brand's multiple video campaigns.

► Quick videos that show, instead of just telling, have contributed to more than 26 million views.

► Videos range from professionally shot commercials (Mayhem campaign) to homegrown compilations (John Riggins' Hometown Hall of Famer video).

LinkedIn

Spruce up your company page.

Company pages offer a platform to share diverse types of content, yet many brands are notably absent on the professional network. Rope your page in, update the cover photo, add boilerplate information, and start sharing. (Here are tips on creating your company page: http://contentmarketinginstitute.com/2011/04/new-linkedin-company-pages-a-step-by-step-guide-for-content-marketers/)

Encourage staff members to stay plugged in.

People who work at your organization (especially execs) can connect their personal profiles to your brand, creating a new source of content that your audience can follow.

Think quality, not quantity.

LinkedIn users tend to be overwhelmed when brands and individuals over-share.

Make sure you're only sharing the highest quality content you create for your brand.

Participate in groups.

Participating in LinkedIn group discussions is a great way to demonstrate thought leadership and strike up conversations that could lead to new business.

Share your content and interact with other group members to establish a strong rapport.

Leverage user-generated content with recommendations.

Bringing in a steady stream of recommendations from clients or customers provides a renewable source of user- generated content. (Need more LinkedIn guidance? Check out tips for using LinkedIn's follow button: http://contentmarketinginstitute.com/2012/02/linkedin-follow-button/)

Who uses LinkedIn well?

Social enterprise software developer Salesforce maintains a clean LinkedIn company page, to which nearly 10,000 employees have connected.

► Page administrators typically post only 2-3 times a day.

► The company's 12 products include 914 recommendations.

Google+

Offer a healthy mix of content media.

Google+ gives you the ability to create an eye-catching page experience. Take advantage of it by posting more than just links and text. Mix in a variety of photos, videos, and infographics for a healthy-looking page.

(Hear from the author of Google+ for Dummies: http://contentmarketinginstitute.com/2011/12/what-google-plus-means-for-marketers/)

Symbols like # and + are your friends.

Hashtags help your posts get discovered through search, while using the + feature gets the attention of individuals and brands. Finding ways to use these tools helps your audience find you.

Share individual content from your staff.

Highlight personalities by pulling in posts from individual staff members to create a social-friendly and personalized experience.

Get more mileage from archived content.
Just because content is old doesn't mean it's outdated. In addition to brand new content, share old and archived content that may be trending or relevant to a timely topic.

Use longer-form content for commentary.

Experiment with expanded posts that feel like mini blog posts. You may want to do this when you're sharing third-party content that could benefit from your spin. (Check out more Google+ content marketing tips: http://contentmarketinginstitute.com/2012/03/google-plus-content-marketing-ideas/)

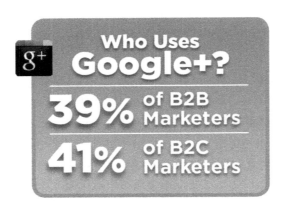

Who uses Google+ well?

Computer hardware brand Dell produces a solid mix of content including videos, pictures, and infographics with corresponding copy.

▶ Consistent updates include at least a few tags to enhance searchability.

▶ Long-form text helps put rich media in perspective by offering some background and commentary.

Pinterest

Decide if the platform fits your audience before jumping in.

As an interest-driven community, Pinterest is geared towards 18-34 year old women. If a good portion of your audience lands in this category, it's a good fit.

It's more than just images.

Videos are powerful (and pin-able). If you have a strong repertoire of video content, use Pinterest to drive traffic back to your website or YouTube channel.

Show your customers some love.

Strengthen relationships, highlight success stories, and drive more traffic by creating a board showing off the achievements of your customers. It's a great way to illustrate your work without much braggadocio.

Share your reading list.

Share book recommendations that are relevant to your audience to establish a stronger bond. Leveraging books that you've actually read helps demonstrate your brand's commitment to constant improvement.

Show your company personality.

Instead of a lone product image or a posed staff picture, show your product or team in action for an image with more personality. Action shots help your audience imagine themselves as a customer or client.

(Find more tips for sharing on Pinterest: http://contentmarketinginstitute.com/2012/07/9-pinterest-board-ideas-for-content-marketers/)

Who uses Pinterest well?

General Electric's "From the Factory Floor" board includes tons of behind-the-scenes content about the company's engineers and technology.

▶ The board mixes picture and video content with great calls to action to repin content.

▶ High-quality content points to other branded social media like YouTube, Facebook, and Flickr.

Foursquare

Encourage your staff to check in at the office and company events.

Create incentives for staff members who check in at work. Do the same for company-sponsored events to highlight your work culture and establish the personal side of your brand.

Do research on your market to fuel content.

Keeping a keen eye on where your audience checks in is a great way to collect data on your target market.

Check in at client and partner meetings.

In addition to company events, encourage executives and other staff members to check in at client and partner meetings to showcase the brands you work with. Some of them may even repay the favor when they visit your office.

Create a badge.

For a fee, Foursquare offers brands the ability to create their own badges. Check-ins and achievements — coupled with users following your brand page — unlock your badge for users trying to win it.

Share tips that are relevant to your audience.

After you've created a brand page, you can share tips with your audience as they're out exploring. When users follow you on Foursquare, they'll have the opportunity to view those tips, creating a compelling content marketing connection.

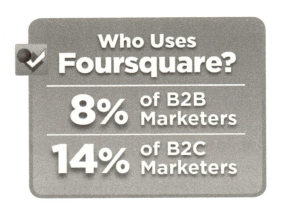

Who uses Foursquare well?

With nearly 65,000 followers, the New York Public Library is a very active organization on Foursquare, sharing tips, specials, and more.

▶ The library shares tips, behind-the-scenes content, and special promotions for events.

▶ Unlocked by 12,000+ people, the Centennial badge is accessible to library followers.

Instagram and Flickr

Post images that accompany your content with a link to the piece.

Coupling images with blog or other website content adds a call to action to your visual stimuli. In this way, picture sharing sites become viable arrows back to your content.

Share unique behind-the-scenes and personal content.

Get personal with your audience; give followers an insider view of the inner workings of your organization. A "behind-the-scenes" feel comes with an exclusivity factor.

Tie promotions to images.

Add promotions to visual content to help with engagement and conversions, and create a call to action that leads followers toward more content.

Turn followers into sources of content.

Ask your followers for pictures that represent your brand, and reward the best contributors with recognition. Offer them a sense of ownership to strengthen the relationship.

Offer high-quality peripheral content.

Even if a topic isn't directly related to your product, service, or brand, if your audience finds it interesting, it's worth sharing. Because Instagram and Flickr are picture-driven, they can open up a whole world of visual possibilities. (Check out more Instagram tips: http://contentmarketinginstitute.com/2012/07/9-pinterest-board-ideas-for-content-marketers/)

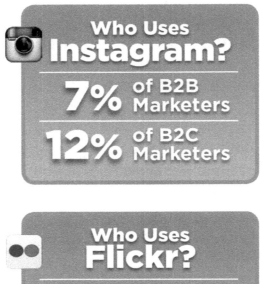

Who uses Instagram and Flickr well?

With around 450,000 followers, Red Bull takes advantage of its extreme sports sponsorships to keep followers engaged.

► Red Bull posts visually stimulating pictures of skaters, snowboarders, and other athletes, reinforcing its brand with the occasional can of Red Bull.

► Hashtags like #givesyouwings are frequently coupled with pictures for better visibility and trending opportunities.

StumbleUpon

Only sign up if you have time to stay active.

Staying active on StumbleUpon is the way to gain more authority for your links. To get organic traffic, sign on, and stumble and rate often.

Use the "paid discovery" service.

StumbleUpon's paid discovery program starts at 10 cents per click, putting your content in front of a targeted audience on the cheap.

Add a StumbleUpon button to each piece of content you create.

Place a Stumble button on your content. A few shares from active users could translate to new, targeted traffic for your content.

Make it easy to share older content, too.

When you add new social channels, it's easy to think of them as part of a new phase in content marketing. But remember, content in your archives can benefit from sharing buttons, too.

Find inspiration for your own content.

Using StumbleUpon often will deliver more relevant content to your doorstep, introducing you to new websites, channels, and brands. As such, you'll find new inspiration for your own content around every corner.

Who uses StumbleUpon well?

Financial management software developer Mint.com signed up for paid discovery with great results.

► Mint.com used layered targeting based on gender and topics like financial planning and self improvement.

► The company's paid-discovery campaign returned a 20 percent increase in site traffic, logging 180,000 monthly visits through StumbleUpon.

Tumblr

Use your tags.

Tag content to help with searchability. Include descriptive tags on each piece of content to give your page much stronger visibility.

Post snippets of content.

Snag an eye-catching quote from a popular post on your blog, include the link and tags, and share the preview.

Other snippets (like pictures) work well to offer a preview of your content before the viewer makes the jump.

Reblog, comment, and like often.

Use these features to share content from other Tumblr users. That way, you reduce some of the burden of content creation while still getting the attention of influencers. You can also create relationships that may result in more people sharing your original content.

Link back to your page.

Attach a link to your Tumblr on every piece of content you post. If content goes viral, users can easily trace it back to your page. Without that link, your content may spiral off, giving you very little ability to track sharing.

Focus your content.

Make sure your content fits a tight niche to help you dominate search results and focus in on the top ways your audience finds you.

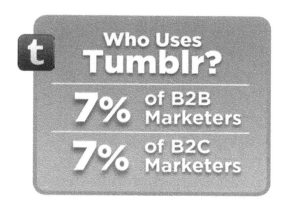

Who uses Tumblr well?

IBM's A Smarter Planet Tumblr page is a well-designed, branded feed of how organizations are spurring innovation.

▶ IBM Tumblr administrators do a lot of reblogging, establishing relationships and reducing the burden of content creation with a curatorial approach.

▶ Each post includes a handful of tags to get more search visibility, drawing in more visitors and notes.

SlideShare

Share your eBooks.

SlideShare offers simpler viewing than a PDF in Adobe Reader, doesn't require a download, is easy to track and measure, and offers a better organic search presence that's independent of your website.

Recycle old content.

Find old PowerPoint presentations and start uploading them. Sales, branding, marketing, and conference presentations are all fair game here. Just make sure to update any outdated content.

Embed your slides on other sites.

Like YouTube, SlideShare gives you the ability to upload a collection of slides to any website. This can be a great way to enhance a blog post or offer a preview of an executive's upcoming conference appearance.

Spend time on your title slides.

The first thing users see is your title slide. Take great care in creating eye-catching, valuable ones to keep viewers from bouncing to another website.

Create lengthy, data-driven presentations.

Longer content tends to perform better on SlideShare. This channel targets a select group of professionals, so keep your content on their radar by driving your presentations with data. (Bonus: Check out more on this tip: http://contentmarketinginstitute.com/2012/07/9-pinterest-board-ideas-for-content-marketers/)

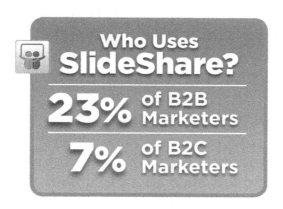

Who uses SlideShare well?

Support desk software developer Help Scout has an active SlideShare presence that uses eBooks to drive traffic back to its website.

▶ Presentations include sleek title pages with phenomenal design throughout.

▶ Slides are numerous and include lots of data to whet the appetites of analytical readers.

Quora

Create a comprehensive profile.

A complete profile enhances the credibility of your questions and answers. It's also a tool that helps point visitors in the right direction when they visit your profile for more info about you and your brand.

Follow topics, and find influencers.

Follow the topics that make the most sense for your brand and your audience. Identify major influencers by viewing who has submitted the most answers.

Ask and answer questions.

This is how you create short-form content that could eventually point back toward your website. It's also a great way to find inspiration for new blog posts, eBooks, videos, or other content topics.

Show your appreciation.

Click the "upvote" and "thank" buttons at the bottom of the post. You'll stay engaged, make a few friends, and help make your content more valuable by identifying high-quality answers.

Develop a board to showcase Q&As your audience may find useful.

Post content to a board of your favorite questions and answers. You can even invite other users to add content to your board, enhancing relationships by collaborating on content.

Who uses Quora well?

SEOmoz founder Rand Fishkin is an extremely active Quora member who garners attention for his business through the site.

▶ Rand maintains a complete profile that highlights his achievements.

▶ He follows topic, answers questions, and upvotes answers he likes, building relationships and keeping his feed fresh.

What is social media?

> *Social computing is not a fad.*
>
> *Nor is it something that will pass you or your company by.*
>
> *Gradually, social computing will impact almost every role, at every kind of company, in all parts of the world.*
>
> Forrester Research, Social Computing
> *How Networks Erode Institutional Power, And What To Do About It*

Introduction

This is a short, sweet summary of the phenomenon called social media. It's an unashamedly straightforward work, intended to give you a brief overview of the story so far, maybe fill in a few gaps and act as a reference guide.

It's intended for anyone, but will be most useful to people working in media, marketing and communications. Things move fast in this world, so this e-book will be updated every now and again.

So how big a deal is social media?

Very big indeed.

To give you an idea of the numbers, when this e-book was last updated there were:

More than **110 million blogs** being tracked by Technorati1, a specialist blog search engine, up from 63 million at the beginning of the year.

An estimated **100 million videos** a day being watched on video sharing website, YouTube

More than **123 million users** on social network Facebook.

What is social media?

Social media is best understood as a group of new kinds of online media, which share most or all of the following characteristics:

Participation

Social media encourages contributions and feedback from everyone who is interested. It blurs the line between media and audience.

Openness

Most social media services are open to feedback and participation. They encourage voting, comments and the sharing of information. There are rarely any barriers to accessing and making use of content – password-protected content is frowned on.

Conversation

Whereas traditional media is about "broadcast" (content transmitted or distributed to an audience) social media is better seen as a two-way conversation.

Community

Social media allows communities to form quickly and communicate effectively. Communities share common interests, such as a love of photography, a political issue or a favorite TV show.

Connectedness

Most kinds of social media thrive on their connectedness, making use of links to other sites, resources and people.

Basic forms of social media

At this time, there are basically six kinds of social media. Note, though, that innovation and change are rife.

Social networks

These sites allow people to build personal web pages and then connect with friends to share content and communication. The biggest social networks are MySpace, Facebook and Bebo.

Blogs

Perhaps the best known form of social media, blogs are online journals, with entries appearing with the most recent first.

Wikis

These websites allow people to add content to or edit the information on them, acting as a communal document or database. The best-known wiki is Wikipedia4, the online encyclopedia which has over 2 million English language articles.

Podcasts

Audio and video files that are available by subscription, through services like Apple iTunes.

Forums

Areas for online discussion, often around specific topics and interests. Forums came about before the term "social media" and are a powerful and popular element of online communities.

Content communities

Communities which organise and share particular kinds of content. The most popular content communities tend to form around photos (Flickr), bookmarked links (del.icio.us) and videos (YouTube).

Microblogging

Social networking combined with bite-sized blogging, where small amounts of content ('updates') are distributed online and through the mobile phone network. Twitter is the clear leader in this field.

Back to the Future

If you think that there's something oddly familiar about descriptions of social media, it may be that you recall some of the discussions in the 1990s about what the web would become. And many of its emerging manifestations are close to the idealistic imaginings from that time.

> **A good way to think about social media is that all of this is actually just about being human beings.**

Sharing ideas, cooperating and collaborating to create art, thinking and commerce, vigorous debate and discourse, finding people who might be good friends, allies and lovers – it's what our species has built several civilisations on. That's why it is spreading so quickly, not because it's great shiny, whizzy new technology, but because it lets us be ourselves – only more so.

And it is in the "more so" that the power of this revolution lies. People can find information, inspiration, like-minded people, communities and collaborators faster than ever before. New ideas, services, business models and technologies emerge and evolve at dizzying speed in social media.

The new means of production and distribution...

Media production

Rather than asking, "Are blogs a fad?" or "How much of this is hype?" it's more useful to look at the fundamentals behind the phenomenal growth of social media.

It used to be that the ability to create content and distribute it to an audience was limited to individuals and organizations that owned the production facilities and infrastructure to do so. In other words: 'the media'.

If you were in the video creation and distribution business you were called a TV station and employed thousands of highly skilled individuals to write, film, edit and broadcast your content through a relatively small number of channels to the public. Similarly, if you were a newspaper, you hired a team of reporters and editors, designers, typesetters, printers and delivery men, and had deals with a network of newsagents for them to sell your product to your audience.

With the advent of digital technology and the internet it became a lot easier for people to create their own content, be it images, words, video or audio. But even five years ago, it was still beyond most people's technical skills to create and maintain their own website.

Today, the ever-lower costs of computers, digital cameras and high-speed internet access, combined with free or low-cost, easy-to-use editing software means that anyone can have a live blog website up and running within minutes of deciding to do so. With a little reading and fiddling they can upload video or sound too.

Distribution...

Production, obviously, is only half of the story. What good is great content unless you can get it to people? Take blogs for instance. People have a limited amount of time to check websites regularly – few people are going to be bothered to check more than a couple of blogs every day.

Now they don't need to. The innovation that has increased the reach of blogs and podcasts and has given terrific impetus to social media's evolution is a technology called RSS (Really Simple Syndication) which allows people to subscribe to a blog or website.

RSS notifies a 'newsreader' or your personal homepage (on, say, Google or Windows Live) that there is new content available and sends it the text and images. You can then read these in your newsreader without having to visit the website itself.

The importance of RSS, therefore, is that it makes it much easier for blogs and other social media to build or become part of communities. They may often be small communities, but to their users they may be highly relevant and valuable.

The other method of distribution that is sometimes neglected in any discussion of social media is search engines. Because blogs are highly connected, in the eyes of Google the more established ones can become an authority on a niche topic.

If, say, you have been blogging about cats for a good few months, and your posts have attracted links from other blogs, then a story about new government legislation on pet ownership on your blog may earn similar ranking for searches on that subject as the local newspaper or even national media.

> It is difficult, indeed dangerous,
> to underestimate the huge changes
> this revolution will bring
> or the power of developing
> technologies to build and destroy
> not just companies but whole
> countries.
> *Rupert Murdoch*

How social media works...

Now let's take a look at each of the main types of social media, and how they work. These explanations are intentionally very general, because with social media every rule seems to have an exception.

In fact, among the defining characteristics of social media are the blurring of definitions, rapid innovation, reinvention and mash-ups.

Each explanation also has a section on how to try out that form of social media yourself, with pointers on both how to find social media that's relevant to you and how you might go about creating it. If you want to really understand how social media works, there's no better way than to take part in it.

Mash-ups

The combination of two or more pieces of content (or software, or websites) is one of the phenomena in social media that make it at once so exciting, fast-moving and sometimes bewildering. Mash-ups are possible because of the openness of social media – many websites and software developers encourage people to play with their services and reinvent them.

There are literally hundreds of mash-ups of the Google Earth service, where people have attached information to parts of the maps. For instance there is a UK rail service mash-up where you can track in real time where trains are on the map. Fans of the TV series 24 have mapped locations from the shows' plotlines on to a Google Earth map.

How social media works...

A popular type of mash-up cannibalizes different pieces of content, typically videos and music. Popular videos on YouTube can spawn hundreds of imitations, homages and (frequently) comic reinterpretations. In communities like this, the number of mash-ups a piece of content spawns is often an indicator of its popularity.

Some marketers have cottoned on to the power of this and encourage people to reinterpret their content.

> ### Three brilliant mash-ups on YouTube:
>
> **8 ½ Mile**
> Eminem + Fellini
>
> **Love Will Freak Us**
> Missy Elliott + Joy Division
>
> **A Hard Day's Night of the Living Dead**
> The Beatles + zombie movies

How social networks work

Social networks on the web are like contained versions of the sprawling blog network. People joining a social network usually create a profile and then build a network by connecting to friends and contacts in the network, or by inviting real-world contacts and friends to join the social network.

These communities retain the interest of their members by being useful to them and providing services that are entertaining or help them to expand their networks.

MySpace, for instance, allows members to create vivid, chaotic home pages (they've been likened to the walls of a teenager's bedroom) to which they can upload images, videos and music.

MySpace has built a lot of its popularity around its music services. There are said to be over three million bands and musicians registered on it, trying to attract a fan base from the 200 million registered accounts. According to Hitwise, in September 2006 MySpace was the 8th largest referrer of traffic to HMV.co.uk, more even than the MSN search engine.

In 2007, **Facebook,** a social network that originated in US colleges, became available for public use in the UK. Its popularity quickly rocketed. Part of Facebook's success is its creators' decision to 'open up' and allow anyone to develop applications and run them on Facebook - without charging them. This has seen Facebook users able to play each other at Scrabble and Chess, compare each others' tastes and send 'virtual gifts', among any number of new ideas vying for attention.

Bebo, which is popular among school-age children, actually has the most members, perhaps helped by the fact that it is grouped around schools and colleges. Crucially, the growth in the use of social networks by young people in recent years has come at the expense of their consumption of traditional media such as TV and magazines. This switch in behaviour was one of the drivers behind the biggest deal in social media to date, when Rupert Murdoch bought MySpace for US $580 million. (BBC http://news.bbc.co.uk/1/hi/business/4695495.stm)

Marketers have also increasingly begun to experiment with trying to reach the members of MySpace and other social networks. Bebo hosts pages for many children's authors for instance, while MySpace has seen a rush of marketing efforts from Toyota to the US Army.

Perhaps the most 'grown-up' of the popular networks is **LinkedIn,** which allows users build their business and professional contacts into an online network. It has been criticised for not being open enough and for charging for too many of its services – but next to Facebook it is still the most popular online social network among people aged 25 and over. The huge success of the 'opening up' of Facebook, as mentioned above, could be a challenge to LinkedIn's 'closed' approach in the future.

How BLOGS WORK

At its simplest, a blog is an online journal where the entries are published with the most recent first. There are a number of features that make blogs noteworthy and different to other websites:

Tone

Blogs tend to be written in a personal, conversational style. They are usually the work of an identified author or group of authors.

Topic

Blogs tend to define what it is they are writing about. They can be as specific as a blog about a book in progress or as wide in scope as „my musings on life and stuff'.

Links and trackbacks

The services people use to write blogs make it very easy for them to insert links to other websites, usually in reference to an article or blog post or to provide further information about the subject they are writing about.

Comments

Each blog post has a comments section, effectively a message board for that article. On blogs with large audiences the debates in these sections can run to hundreds of comments at a time.

Subscription

Blogs can be subscribed to, usually via RSS technology, making it easy to keep up with new content. Blogs are easy to set up using any of a number of services. One of the simplest is the free Blogger service from Google. Others such as Wordpress and TypePad offer more features, the latter for a fee.

Different types of blogs

With millions of people around the world of different ages and backgrounds blogging about whatever they feel like, it is about as easy to generalise about 'bloggers' as it is to make sweeping statements about 'human beings'.

Here are some of the main kinds of blogs you will come across:

Personal blogs

Many millions of people keep blogs about their everyday lives, much like public diaries. These sometimes become very popular indeed, especially those anonymous, slightly risque ones. You know the sort: they get written about in the Sunday Times and become best-selling novels. One of the best-known personal blogs is Dooce.

Political blogs

Especially in the US, but increasingly in the UK, blogs are being written about politics. Often perceived as a response to media bias (across the political spectrum) they tend to comment on the news, giving closer analysis of issues they feel have been misrepresented or glossed over by mainstream media.

In America most if not all of the contenders for the presidency in 2008 already have bloggers on staff to advise on reaching political bloggers and their readers. We are not quite at that stage in the UK, but blogging has been playing a part in the resurgence of grassroots Conservative politics, and right-of-centre bloggers such as Iain Dale and Guido Fawkes have been making their presence in the UK mainstream media. Influential examples from the political left include MediaLens and Harry's Place.

Business blogs

Many professionals and businesses now have blogs. They can allow companies to communicate in a less formal style than has been traditional in newsletters, brochures and press releases, which can help to give a human face and voice to the organisation. For individuals in business a blog can become a very effective way of building a network of like-minded individuals and raising their own profiles. Blog Maverick is a good example.

'Almost media' blogs

Some blogs are unashamedly media businesses in their own right, taking advertising and employing a blogger or a group of bloggers full-time. Effectively, they are startups that are taking advantage of the new blogging technologies and opportunities to build communities of readers in new or niche subject areas. These are generally to be found covering news and opinion in the technology and media industries. Try Businesspundit.com or Hecklerspray.

Mainstream media blogs

Most national newspapers in the UK – not to mention the BBC – now have blogs for some of their reporters and editors. These can provide useful insights into the news gathering and reporting process, but will also give vent to personal views that the journalist may otherwise have kept to themselves. For example, see BBC business editor Robert Peston's blog. It's worth noting that while many journalist blogs are hosted on newspaper sites themselves, a large number are independent, personal blogs with a major focus on their professional interests.

Reading Blogs

The easiest way to read blogs is to subscribe to ones you find interesting using the Bloglines, Google Reader or Newsgator newsreader services. A newsreader is a website or piece of software where you can go to read a newsfeed that you are subscribed to via RSS. All blogs and most news websites have RSS feeds attached to them.

You can find blogs on topics that you're interested in by using search engines like Technorati or Google Blog Search. If you find a blog which is particularly interesting or relevant to you, have a look for its 'blogroll' (list of recommended blogs) – it's a great way of exploring the networks of blogs.

How WIKIS WORK

Wikis are websites that allow people to contribute or edit content on them. They are great for collaborative working, for instance creating a large document or project plan with a team in several offices. A wiki can be as private or as open as the people who create it want it to be.

Wikipedia

The most famous wiki is of course Wikipedia, an online encyclopaedia that was started in 2001. It now has over 2.5 million articles in English alone and over a million members. (Wikipedia http://en.wikipedia.org/wiki/Main_Page)

In 2005 the respected scientific journal Nature conducted a study into the reliability of the scientific entries in Wikipedia and Encyclopaedia Britannica. No one was surprised that Encyclopaedia Britannica was the more reliable of the two – what was remarkable was that it was only marginally more accurate. The Encyclopedia Britannica team issued a 20-page rebuttal of the study a few months later. Others observed that while Encyclopaedia Britannica had no entries for wiki, Wikipedia has a 2,500 word article on Encyclopaedia Britannica, its history and methodology. But Wikipedia is more than a reference source. During a major breaking news story, especially one which affects large numbers of people directly, such a natural disaster or political crisis, Wikipedia acts as a collective reporting function. (Nature http://www.nature.com/nature/journal/v438/n7070/full/438900a.html)

Trying out wikis...

Everyone knows Wikipedia, here are some other examples of large wiki projects that you can take a look at and even participate in:

Wikia

A community of wikis on different subjects

wikiHow

A practical 'how to' manual for everything from making coffee to writing business plans

Wikinews

Wikipedia's news project. You can start your own public wiki in the Wikia community, or look at the technology's possibilities for team working by trying out the services from companies like JotSpot and Socialtext.

How PODCASTS WORK

Podcasts are audio or video files that are published on the internet and that users can subscribe to. Sometimes 'vodcast' is used to specifically describe video services. It is the subscription feature that makes a podcast so powerful as a form of social media. People have long been able to upload audio content to the web, but the subscription feature means that people can build regular audiences and communities around their shows. It effectively puts private individuals or brands on a level playing field with traditional media organisations when it comes to competing for people's attention with AV content online.

Podcasts, like personal video recorders (PVRs), are part of a shift in media consumption patterns, which increasingly sees people watching or listening to content when and where it suits them. This is sometimes known as time-shifting. When a new podcast is posted to the web, all the subscribers' podcast services (such as iTunes) are automatically notified and download the programme to their computer's hard drive. The podcast can then be either listened to on the computer or downloaded onto an MP3 player, such as an iPod.

Naturally the advent of the podcast has also meant that media brands have been able to invade one another's traditional territory. Many national newspapers in the UK have started effectively producing their own radio-style programmes and distributing them via their previously text-and-picture based websites. Channel 4 has also launched its own audio/podcasting brand, 4Radio.

> ### *Getting started with podcasts*
>
> If you already have an iPod and use iTunes you can click on the Podcast icon in the left-hand toolbar to access podcasts and subscribe to them.
>
> Other good places to find and start listening to podcasts are **Podcast Alley** and **Yahoo!**
>
> **Podcasts**
> If you fancy trying your hand at creating your own podcast, download the free audio editing tool **Audacity** or have a look at the 'how to' guide at **wikiHow.**

How FORUMS WORK

Internet forums are the longest established form of online social media. They most commonly exist around specific topics and interests, for example cars or music. Each discussion in a forum is known as a thread, and many different threads can be active simultaneously.

This makes forums good places to find and engage in a variety of detailed discussions. They are often built into websites as an added feature, but some exist as stand-alone entities. Forums can be places for lively, vociferous debate, for seeking advice on a subject, for sharing news, for flirting, or simply for whiling away time with idle chat. In other words, their huge variety reflects that of face-to-face conversations.

The sites are moderated by an administrator, whose role it is to remove unsuitable posts or spam. However, a moderator will not lead or guide the discussion. This is a major difference between forums and blogs. Blogs have a clear owner, whereas a forum's threads are started by its members.

Forums have a strong sense of community. Some are very enclosed, existing as 'islands' of online social activity with little or no connection to other forms of social media. This may be because forums were around long before the term 'social media' was coined, and in advance of any of the other types of community we associate with the term.

In any event, they remain hugely popular, often with membership in the hundreds of thousands. Forum search engine BoardTracker monitors over 61 million conversation threads across almost 40,000 forums, and it is by no means a comprehensive index. (Boardtracker http://www.boardtracker.com/)

How CONTENT COMMUNITIES WORK

Content communities look a bit like social networks – you have to register, you get a home page and you can make connections with friends. However, they are focussed on sharing a particular type of content.

For example, Flickr is based around sharing photography and is the most popular service of its kind in the UK. Members upload their photos to the site and choose whether to make them public or just share with family and friends in their network.

Thousands of groups have formed on Flickr around areas of common interest. There are groups dedicated to particular graffiti artists, towns, sports and animals. If you work for a reasonably well-known brand it is worth taking a look to see if there is a Flickr group about you – there are groups for motorbike brands, consumer electronics brands and even the cult notebook brand Moleskine. As testament to its enormous success, Flickr was bought by Yahoo! in 2005 for an estimated US $30 million. (CNN http://money.cnn.com/magazines/business2/business2 _archive/2005/12/01/8364623/)

YouTube is the world's largest video sharing service, with over 100 million videos viewed every day. Members of YouTube can upload videos or create their own "channels" of favourite videos. The viral nature of YouTube videos is enhanced by a feature that makes it easy for people to cut and paste videos hosted by YouTube directly into their blogs.

As well as thousands of short films from people's own video cameras, webcams and camera phones, there are many clips from TV shows and movies hosted on the service. Some people also use the service to record video blogs.

YouTube started as a small private company, but was bought by Google for $1.65 billion in October 2006. (YouTube http://news.bbc.co.uk/1/hi/business/6034577.stm)

Digg is a news and content community. Members submit links to news stories that they think will be of interest and these are voted on by other members. Once a story has garnered about a critical number of votes (the number varies according to how busy the site is) it will be moved to the front page where it will receive wider attention from members as well as more casual visitors to the site.

Digg claims to receive 20 million unique visitors every month, and certainly the volume of traffic via popular links from the service is so great that it can cause smaller companies' servers to crash.

As with other social media platforms, rumours of acquisition deals and massive valuations for the service are flying around, but it remains independent and relatively small in terms of the number of employees (around 40).

Folksonomies

Content communities often display characteristics of what are known as folksonomies. The term folksonomy refers to the way that information is organised – it is a play on the word taxonomy, a classification system.

In a folksonomy the information or content is "tagged" with one-word descriptors. Anyone can add a tag to a piece of content and see what other people have tagged, too. For instance, del.icio.us, a bookmark-sharing service that replaces the favourites folder on your web browser, is a prime example of a folksonomy. Content communities such as Flickr, YouTube and blogs generally make use of the folksonomy approach of tagging content to make it more easily found.

Music folksonomies have proved particularly popular. Services such as last.fm let you tag tracks as you listen to them, and search and link to music based on other people's tags.

How MICRO-BLOGGING WORKS

Micro-blogging is tool that combines elements of blogging with instant messaging and social networking.

The clear leader in the micro-blogging field is Twitter with over 1 million users. (Tech Crunch http://www.techcrunch.com/2008/04/29/end-of-speculation-the-real-twitter-usage-numbers/)

Other notable micro-blogging players include Pownce and Jaiku, which offer various different features, but for the purposes of this e-book it makes sense to focus on the Twitter format.

Twitter users can send messages of up to 140 characters instantly to multiple platforms. 90% of Twitter interactions are not made via the Twitter website, but via mobile text message, Instant Messaging, or a desktop application such as Twitterific. Its flexibility is further enhanced by the ability to subscribe to updates via RSS. (D.Construct http://dconstruct07.backnetwork.com/feeds/default.as px?listtype=full&contributor=philwhitehouse)

Uses of Twitter vary. It's popular among homeworkers and freelancers, who use it in part as a 'virtual watercooler'. Other people use it simply to stay in touch with a close network and share thoughts or start conversations.

Its suitability as a vehicle for breaking news has encouraged the BBC and CNN to introduce Twitter feeds. Even candidates for the US Presidency have taken to Twitter (for example, Barack Obama).

An important feature to note is that Twitter can be indexed via Google. As with so much on the web, it's a public platform, so it's worth remembering that as such your use of it may become part of your 'permanent record'.

How SECOND LIFE WORKS

One of the biggest online marvels to capture the imagination of the traditional media is Second Life. It's an online computer game, but is perhaps better understood as an online virtual world. By registering and downloading the software, you can enter the game world and create an 'avatar' – an in-game representation of yourself.

Since Second Life encourages community and social interaction, some consider it to be a form of social media, although like so much in the new forms of online media it could very well be considered as a category of its own.

More than 10 million Second Life user accounts have been created, and around 1.5 million residents log in to the virtual world every month. Over 1 million US dollars are spent in Second Life each day. (Reuters http://secondlife.reuters.com/)

That last figure, perhaps the most surprising to those unfamiliar with Second Life, is down to the functioning economy that exists in the virtual world. This is made possible by the ability to own private property within the game and by setting an exchange rate between the game's currency and the US dollar (approximately 270 "Linden dollars" to the US dollar). In fact, Second Life created its first millionaire in November 2006, when Anshe Chung amassed virtual assets worth one million US dollars.

Marketers are beginning to experiment with the game world too. Toyota has launched in-game models to promote its 'Scion' range, while Peugeot has invited gamers to try a recent model on a virtual racetrack, built to coincide with the Frankfurt Motor Show.

During its 2006 Big Weekend festival, BBC Radio 1 had a stage in Second Life with avatars of presenters and bands performing – anyone visiting the concert received a virtual digital radio that they could listen to Radio 1 on in the virtual world. Doubtless a large part of the marketing benefit from these in-game presences really comes from the publicity in the non-virtual world that these generate, but these are intriguing precedents for marketers.

what next?

Whether we are still using **MySpace** or **Second Life** in two, five or ten year's time is anyone's guess. The unique way that the internet continually improves in response to user experience is driving innovation on an unprecedented scale.

There will no doubt be exciting new variants on current formats, and perhaps innovations that come to be thought of as new forms of social media. They will develop in response to our appetite for new ways to communicate and to the increasingly flexible ways that we can go online. That's the detail – impossible to predict. What is beyond doubt is that social media – however it may be referred to in the future – is a genie that will not be disappearing back into its bottle.

GLOSSARY

Term

Blog Originally 'web log' a website where the most recent entries appear first, typically allowing users to subscribe to updates and to leave comments.

Bookmarks, bookmarking Saving an item, page or website for future reference, increasingly via an online account such as del.icio.us. Works in a similar way to the 'favourites' feature of a web browser.

Communities Online networks that exist around shared interests or shared content.

Content communities Communities which organise around and share particular kinds of content. Popular content communities exist around photos (Flickr), bookmarked links (del.icio.us), news (Digg) and videos (YouTube).

Instant Messaging (IM) A form of real-time communication via the internet between two or more people based on typed text, for example Google Talk.

Mash-up A hybrid web application combining content from two or more different data sources, for example data added to Google Maps.

Micro-blogging Instant publishing of bite-size amounts of content via a service such as Twitter.

RSS (Really Simple SYNDICATION)
A method of subscribing to a site's content and being alerted to new updates without visiting the site, either through the user's web browser or an RSS aggregator (for example Bloglines).

SECOND LIFE The best-known 'virtual world', in which users can move around and interact with one another and the environment as 3D characters (avatars).

SOCIAL MEDIA Media that users can easily participate in, share and create content for, including blogs, social networks, wikis, forums and virtual worlds.

SOCIAL NETWORKS Channels through which individuals can interact socially. Successful online examples include Facebook, MySpace and Bebo

TAGS, TAGGING Keywords that label pieces of content (for instance blog posts, bookmarks) and make them easy to organise and search.

TECHNORATI RANKING A blog's authority, as measured by blog tracking website Technorati.

TWITTER A micro-blogging service that distributes bitesized chunks of text across multiple platforms, including mobile, instant messaging and email. Messages are often status updates about what a user is doing.

VIRTU AL WORLDS An online environment in which people can interact with each other and the environment as 3D characters (avatars).

VODCAST Video files that are published on the internet and can be subscribed to, a derivative of podcasts (audio files).

USEFUL WEBSITES

Apple iTunes http://www.apple.com/itunes/
Audacious http://audacious-media-player.org/
Bebo http://www.bebo.com/
Blogger https://www.blogger.com/start
Bloglines http://www.bloglines.com/
Boardtracker http://www.boardtracker.com/
del.icio.us http://del.icio.us/
Digg http://digg.com/
Facebook http://www.facebook.com
Flickr http://www.flickr.com/
4Radio https://www.channel4radio.com/
Google Blog Search http://blogsearch.google.com/
Google Earth http://earth.google.com/
Google Talk http://www.google.com/talk/
iCrossing http://www.icrossing.com/
Jaiku http://www.jaiku.com/
JotSpot http://www.jot.com/
Last.fm http://www.last.fm/
LinkedIn http://www.linkedin.com/
MySpace http://www.myspace.com/
Newsgator http://www.newsgator.com/home.aspx
Open http://open.typepad.com/open/
Podcast Alley http://www.podcastalley.com/
Pownce http://www.pownce.com/
Rojo http://www.rojo.com/today/
SearchSense http://www.iCrossing.com/search-sense/
Second Life http://secondlife.com/
Socialtext http://www.socialtext.com/

iCrossing http://www.iCrossing.com/
Technorati http://technorati.com/
Twitter http://twitter.com/
Twitterific http://iconfactory.com/software/twitterrific
TypePad http://www.typepad.com/
Wikia http://www.wikia.com/wiki/Wikia
wikiHow http://www.wikihow.com
Wikinews http://en.wikinews.org/wiki/Main_Page
Wikipedia http://en.wikipedia.org/wiki/Main_Page
Windows Live http://home.live.com/?mkt=en-gb
Wordpress http://wordpress.org/
Yahoo! Podcasts http://podcasts.yahoo.com/
YouTube http://www.youtube.com/

Social Media Marketing

Introduction

Social media can be leveraged to create wonderful marketing masterpieces. Big name companies like Skittles and Dell have successfully used social media to increase their sales, brand, and the community around their products. Small companies like Kogi BBQ are using social media to increase their sales and dominate the late night food craze in Los Angeles. No matter your company size, social media can be used to start a conversation with your target market and elevate your brand.

SEOP's Social Media Consulting Team has successfully worked for clients and built strong campaigns that drive traffic and build community. Through our experience, we have developed the proprietary 5 Pillar Model that teaches our clients how to use social media for business and how to execute the strategies that we develop together.

This is your guide to the 5 Pillars of social media marketing, and how you can leverage social media for your company's success:

Pillar 1: What is Social Media? – We breakdown social media marketing into its core components so that you can understand the fundamentals. Social Media is about building a conversation with your clients and consumers.

Pillar2: Common Mistakes Companies Make With Social Media – Though you may understand social media and have a solid foundation to build on top of, it is still possible to fall into the common pitfalls and mistakes that most companies make. Avoid the crucial mistakes and you'll be well positioned for social media success.

Pillar 3: The Different Ways Companies Use Social Media – Now that you understand the common pitfalls, it's time to take a look at the companies that get it right. Companies are successfully using social media to drive sales, build traffic, hire employees, build a community, and create a positive, well-known brand.

Pillar4: A Framework for Developing a Social Media Strategy – The strategy development portion of a social media campaign is crucial for the success of a company. You must ask and answer the appropriate and relevant questions to develop the right campaign: What social sites are your target market currently using? How much time is needed to consistently interact with your social community?

Pillar5: How toMeasure Return on Investment – Strategy and research are of course only half the battle. Once your strategy is set, it's time to execute by either building a team, training your current team, or hiring outside consultants to implement. This is by far the most important part of social media marketing so it is of the utmost importance that you get it right.

Pillar 1: What is Social Media?

I know that you're ready to jump right in and start building a social media strategy. Before we do this, it is essential that you understand what social media is and why so many people are using it. Let's start with a definition. According to Wikipedia,

"Social media is online content created by people using highly accessible and scalable publishing technologies. At its most basic sense, social media is a shift in how people discover, read and share news, information and content. It's a fusion of sociology and technology, transforming monologues (one too many) into dialogues (many to many) and is the democratization of information, transforming people from content readers into publishers. Social media has become extremely popular because it allows people to connect in the online world to form relationships for personal, political and business use."

Wow, that's a lot of information! So let's break it down into its 3 main components: publishing, information diffusion, and relationship building.

Social Media: A Publishing Technology for Everyone

Social media is unlike any other technology in history. It has created a modern-day renaissance for several reasons, which are broken down here:

Social media is online

Social media is something that takes place online. It is a type of communication that takes place outside of in-person meetings, phone calls, or foot traffic. That means social media is location-independent, which makes it a valuable part of any company's business strategy.

Social media is user-generated

Content used to be something that very few people created. Reporters, TV anchors, movie directors, authors, radio DJs, and magazine editors created content, and everyone else consumed it. Now, everyone is a publisher, and the people who use the content are also the ones who create it.

Social media is highly accessible and scalable

Social media is highly accessible and scalable to the public, which means that social media has lots of users and offers plenty of opportunity for companies. Because social media is easy to access, the tools for social media are easy and intuitive enough for the common person to use. Even if you don't use social media now, there's no reason not to jump in!

Social Media: A Way to Diffuse Information

No other existing media is capable of diffusing information faster than social media. Here's why:

Social media is a shift in how people discover, read, and share news, media, and content

Television and newspapers areno longer king when it comes to filtering and sharing news. People are more likely to get their news by reading Trending Topics on Twitter, and they are more likely to share a link to a friend's blog post than MSN's homepage.

Social media is a fusion of sociology and technology

Social media is user-controlled, which means that sociologic components play a large role in any company's social media business strategy. The limits of social media are only set by the limits of the technology of social media tools.

Social media is a dialogue

At one time, companies had a monologue with its customers. Companies put out television commercials or print ads about its products and waited to see whether the sales rolled in to determine success rates. Now, social media allows companies to have a dialogue with its customers and gain valuable feedback and input as it creates the message.

Social media is the democratization of information

Information and messaging for a company was once controlled by its marketing and sales departments. Now, with the democratization of information, no one owns the message about a product or company. Every company must become part of the conversation or risk letting users become the voice of the company.

Social Media: A Way to Build Relationships by Sharing

Humans are interesting in that the way they build relationships is through sharing. It may be sharing something that happened in their personal lives, or it may be sharing something funny on TV. Sharing is an essential component of social media, so let's break it down into parts:

Social media is people connecting with others

Social media allows each person to connect with others, which means most of the messaging a person receives is from his or her network. It's essential for companies to learn to network with its customers in order to promote the company message.

Social media is content readers become content publishers

Content readers are not only consumers. Social media allows content readers to become content publishers. In this way, social media allows content readers to share the content with their own network of followers by publishing or republishing the message in their own words.

Social media is forming relationships for personal, political, and business use

Social media is not just about content or messaging in a different format. Social media is about relationships. For companies, social media is about creating a more personal relationship with end-consumers to build a network around a service or product.

It is clear that there are many components to social media, but the best way to understand social media is to just try it. I hope by now you're excited to see what social media can do for your business!

Pillar 2: Common Mistakes Companies Make With Social Media

Now that we've talked about social media, it's important to note what social media is not. This is best answered by talking about the common mistakes companies make with social media.These mistakes fall into three categories: mistakes with strategy, mistakes with tools, and mistakes with messaging. Most of these mistakes are easily avoidable if a company is willing to take time to understand the users' wants and needs on each medium.

Common Mistakes Companies Make With Strategy

Some of the most common mistakes companies make with social media revolve around making decisions that aren't consistent with having good business sense. Because social media tools are free, some companies tend to take the pasta approach: throwing noodles at a wall to see what sticks. Here are some of the most common mistakes to avoid with social media strategy:

Not developing a social media strategy

Because social media is the hottest trend in marketing, companies assume that all they have to do is set up a Twitter account and a Facebook fan page. This is the equivalent of pulling random magazines out of off the rack and purchasing full page color ad in each one, then throwing together a quick and dirty PowerPoint flyer to run. Just like any other communication medium, social media requires a well-thought out marketing strategy plan.

Even though a social media strategy is important, don't wait for the strategy to set up your company's accounts. Reserving your company's name on various social media sites is of the utmost importance. Furthermore, because it takes time to build social media accounts, every minute you waste by not being there is followers you could be losing.

Gathering followers rather than building a network

There are no shortcuts in social media, and the bottom line is companies have to build relationships with their customers before they can sell anything. Social media may seem free, but the hidden time costs to build relationships Social media is not a quick way to make more sales; in fact, social media actually adds cycle time to the sales process. Just like any other process, a company must consider how much of its resources to invest.

Putting all eggs in one basket

It's exciting to see extraordinary results on one form of social media, and tempting to invest all your resources into what's working. Try to resist. With the speed at which technology changes, social media is starting to look similar to the fashion cycle: one day you're in, the next day you're out. Tools fall in and out of fashion all the time – remember Friendster, and more recently, MySpace? Companies that build a large equity on one tool will find themselves with nothing if the tool loses popularity.

Putting the horse before the carriage

Another cliché is the company that doesn't follow a logical process with social media and then wonders why it isn't seeing results. Common sense comes in handy here. For example, consider a company that doesn't currently have many customers, but creates a Facebook fan page and starts promoting it with Facebook ads. The keyword is "fan;" people who haven't experienced the product are not likely to join a fan club for it. Make sure your company is following a logical customer acquisition process by thinking about social media from the user-perspective.

Common Mistakes Companies Make With Social Media Tools

Social media is not a set of tools, but rather a way to communicate information. Here are some of the most common mistakes companies make in regards to social media tools:

Thinking the tools are everything

Most social media talk revolves around tools – i.e.: 10 Ways to Get More Followers on Twitter. While it's useful to get into the details and tactics of social media, a solid marketing strategy should work no matter the medium. The smartest companies will focus on strategy because in the world of Web 2.0, the tools are constantly changing.

Not using the tools correctly

It takes a long time to build credibility, especially as a company because individuals are taught to be wary of anything that looks like marketing or spamming. Unfortunately, it only takes one discrepancy to do damage to a company's reputation. Err on the side of caution with each tool, and take time to listen to the conversations and learn the etiquette for each medium.

Not using the tools at all

Every tool holds opportunity for companies, so companies must be willing to experiment. Rest assured your competitors will be experimenting, so don't let them set the tone or build equity without having your own presence.

Common Mistakes Companies Make With Messaging

Every social media user has a very clear idea of what social media means to them, and how they want to be approached by companies on social media. Most companies don't realize that the way they approach social media sends its own message to consumers. Here are some of the most common mistakes companies make with messaging:

Creating impersonal accounts

Users don't follow companies; they follow engaging people who work at companies. Unless the tool is meant specifically for companies to use (i.e.: Facebook fan pages), every account should be an actual person who has a name and a title that clearly signifies him or her as a face of the company. This person should write with a conversational tone and respond to other participants in the conversation. Automated accounts or accounts that are updated with a stream of links do not produce results.

Controlling the message

Social media is not about controlling a message. In fact, the very nature of social media is such that no one person or organization can control the message. Because social media is a medium to share information through a network, companies must realize that once they put the message out there, they have no control anymore. Users can choose to edit the message, inject their own opinions into the message, share the message, or ignore the message. Furthermore, companies can't even control where the message starts: a user can also create a message about a company without having any affiliation to them. Because of the nature of social media, companies that try to control the message will have difficulty reaping any of the benefits of the medium.

Not controlling the message

While companies should be careful about trying to exercise too much control over the message, there is also the opposite end of the spectrum to avoid. Companies often cite "control over message" as a reason not to participate in social media, but the truth is that companies have lost control of the message whether they participate or not. This is because, as mentioned earlier, users can create a message and drive the conversation surrounding that message.

So how can companies exercise some control over a message and still reap the benefits of social media (rapid diffusion of information through people sharing messages with their networks)? The answer is that companies need to participate in the conversation. Responding to complaints and stressing the benefits and what the company does well; these are all ways for companies to control the end-consumer's perception of its products.

Abusing permission

Abusing permission is by far one of the worst mistakes a company can make with messaging. An example would be if a company collected emails from various blogs in a certain niche and started sending weekly newsletters. While this seems harmless on the surface, none of these bloggers signed up for the company's weekly emails, and thus have not requested the information.

Abusing permission is a fast way for companies to lose credibility, damage relationships, and generally make a bad name for themselves in social media. So where do you draw the line with abusing permission?

Unfortunately, this question is similar to asking where comedians draw the line with potentially offensive jokes. The truth is that different users have different levels of tolerance. Just like a comedian might experiment with messaging based on the feedback he or she is receiving from the audience, your company must experiment with the right level of communication, erring on the side of unobtrusive.

Worried about making these mistakes? As long as you follow along with this book, you can rest easy that you're doing everything right with social media.

Pillar 3: The Different Ways Some Companies Use Social Media

There are several reasons your company has decided to use social media. For some companies, it's to improve relationships and communication internally, while other companies use social media to recruit employees to the company. Most companies are interested in using social media to improve the bottom line. Here are some of the benefits social media can lend your company in each of these situations:

Using social media internally

Social media can be used internally to improve communication across business functions and help your employees build a sense of camaraderie around the office. It's also a useful method for collaborating quickly and independent of location. Yet another use of social media is documenting conversations, discussions, and decisions to be used later in performance reviews or decision case studies.

The benefits of using social media beyond its usage mainly revolve around costs. For a start-up or a small to mid-sized business, social media may be a very cost-effective solution to other software packages on the market. Many of the typical social media tools have closed-network business solution counterparts. For example, the business version of Twitter is an application called Yammer, and like Twitter, it's free to use.

As with any decision to use with social media, the decision to use social media as an internal solution depends on the company's goals and resource constraints.

Using social media to reach potential employees

Human resources professionals use social media to build the employer brand of the company and sell the company as a preferred place of employment. Human resources professionals use social media to monitor their company's brand for damage control. With websites like The Vault and PayScale allowing employees to "tell-all" about their former jobs, brand management is more important than ever for HR professionals. Finally, they can also use social media to research candidates and learn more about them beyond what is featured on a resume or in a cover letter.

Similar to using social media internally, using social media to recruit potential employees is cost-effective. Rather than purchasing expensive postings on Monster or CareerBuilder, human resources professionals can post the job requisite on LinkedIn. Human resources professionals have formed several online groups to discuss HR issues, provide general career advice to hopeful job candidates or professionals dealing with difficult situations.

Using social media to reach end-consumers

There are so many ways to use social media to communicate with the customer, and as social media goes mainstream companies are finding new ways every day. All of these purposes for communication fall into three main functions: public relations and marketing, sales, and customer services. Each of these three usages will be discussed in detail at a later point.

Before your company goes any further with social media, it's important to decide what the goal is. Your company may want to use social media for one, two, or all three of these purposes, and the strategies and tactics for each purpose are different. For the remainder of this book, we will primarily discuss strategy and tactics for using social media to reach customers; however, the frameworks and case studies may be adapted to suit any other needs your company may have for social media.

Pillar 4: A Framework for Developing Your Company's Social Media Strategy

Just like every startup should have some form of a business plan, every company embarking into the world of social media should have some form of a social media strategy. While the tools used to achieve results on social media are important, they are merely objects in a toolkit. Ultimately, tricks and hacks for various social media tools are merely tactics to achieve a strategy; that's why we start with the strategy and then dive into the tools.

The framework for developing a social media strategy consists of threepotential functions: public relations and marketing, sales, and customer services.

PR and Marketing

Customer Services

Sales

Social media can be used to further goals within just one of these three functions, two these functions, or a company could use social media to satisfy the needs of all three of these functions. These three functions feed each other in a cycle, and companies can create a fairly comprehensive social media strategy by taking each into consideration.

Public Relations and Marketing

This section talks specifically about using social media to build brand awareness and as a viral marketing tool. In this section, you'll find answers to questions like:

How do I find my audience?

How do I get the word out?

What is a viral marketing campaign?

What are the components of a viral marketing campaign?

What are some tricks that help sites, posts, and videos go viral?

Brand Awareness

If your company is small, brand awareness is one of the most important and difficult things you can do. The only way to create brand awareness on social media is to find your audience and get the word out!

Find your audience

Very few social media tools will work for every company; however, if your company is just starting out with social media, you can find plenty of people by sticking to the biggest social media sites. Generally, the strategy for finding an audience is looking for groups of people with similar interests to keywords that make sense for your company. The following places are a great place to start looking for your audience:

Facebook and MySpace (and any social networking sites) – Look for your audience by searching for groups that are directly related to your product or service. You can also look for fan pages that are related to your competitors' products or services. For example, if your company sold vampire teeth, you might look at fans of the Twilight series. The same techniques you use for Facebook also work for MySpace, except MySpace uses groups and does not have fan pages.

Twitter (and any social messaging utilities) – Look up each of your competitors on Twitter – the people following your competitors are likely going to be interested in your Twitter feed as well. Similarly, people following anyone with the same topics as you are potential followers. For example, if you are marketing sports products, a company that sells college recruiting services to athletes would be a good audience. You can also use keyword searches at http://search.twitter.com to find people who are tweeting about your keywords.

Google and Yahoo groups (and any email list groups) – Google groups is a wonderful place to find your audience. Furthermore, each of Google's groups comes with an email list and you can send emails and messages to the members of the group. Yahoo has a similar service with similar features.

Ning or MeetUp (and any user-created social networking sites) – Ning is an underutilized resource for finding an audience. Often, you can find fan sites or sites built around products and services that are similar to yours. Furthermore, Ning is a great place for companies to create a presence around their products.

MeetUp is slightly different in that it allows people to network with people in their area that they meet online. MeetUp is wonderful tool for finding an audience locally, or by location, and/or organizing company-sponsored events.

LinkedIn (and any professional networking sites) – LinkedIn is a great resource for individuals marketing services or companies that market primarily B2B. You can find groups and subgroups based around interests, professional function, and/or companies. There is also LinkedIn Answers where you can answer questions from potential clients and build a following that way.

StumbleUpon, Digg, and Del.icio.us (and any social bookmarking sites) –You can find an audience on StumbleUpon by looking for people who are subscribed to your keywords. Digg also divides its link submissions into categories, which can be found at the top of every page. Del.icio.us is a bookmarking site that allows users to create their own tagging system, so you can find people by searching tags for your keywords.

AllTop and Technorati (and any blog tracking sites) – AllTop has a search function that allows you to find topical pages that list all the blogs within that topic. Technorati sorts blogs by user-defined tags as well. Search for your keywords on these two sites to find all the bloggers who write about your topic – each will have build a community of people around their blogs.

Get the word out

When it's time to get the word out, your company must communicate clearly what it's all about. Here are some questions to consider:

How will your product or service help the end-consumer?

What are the features of your product or service?

What are the benefits of using your product or service

How is your product an improvement over other solutions or ways of doing things?

How is your product or service different from direct competitors?

What can the end-consumer gain by connecting with your company via social media?

Too often, companies believe that everyone understands what their product or service does, when really that's not the case. Social media is a medium where you may encounter people who are not in your industry or have never seen your product, especially if it's a new invention. If your company can find a way to answer these questions on social media, the company will get much higher brand awareness because people are more likely to share information that they understand.

Viral Marketing

Most companies have heard of the benefits of viral marketing using social media, but few understand how to execute a viral marketing campaign. First, let's answer the question: What is a viral marketing campaign?

There's a common misconception that viral marketing messages must have millions of page views or attract hundreds of thousands of followers in a short period of time in order to be successful. Unfortunately, very few small to mid-sized companies will ever see this type of success because its market is too small or its products are focused on a niche. Viral marketing campaigns are simply compelling messages that exploit common behaviors and utilize existing networks, that can be transferred effortlessly from person to person on a large scale. The measures of success of a viral marketing campaign must take into account the competitors, resources, and niche of the company.

Now that you know what a viral marketing strategy is, you may be asking: what makes sites, posts, and videos go viral? There are three components behind every viral marketing campaign, and without at least some of each of these three components, success is unlikely. These three components are a large user base, a remarkable message, and a compelling reason to share that message.

Component 1: Building a Large User Base

There are only two ways to get a message to a large group of people: invest a lot of time, or invest a lot of money. If your company is interested in social media, it's probably because you want to reach a large user base without having to shell out a lot of cash.

One thing to remember about social media is that it's not "free." Most of the tools are free, and there is a lot of free content explaining how to use social media for your company. Unfortunately, the reality of social media is that it takes *time*; much more time than, say, creating a banner advertisement. For companies with several employees, time costs money as well.

The good news is that there is no better time to start than today. There are some simple principles to building an online presence on several different networks, and with just a small investment of time each day, you can leverage social media for your business.

Sign-up – This seems so obvious, yet so many companies don't even create accounts on the biggest social networks. Even if your company isn't yet confident with what it wants to do with social media, there is no reason not to have, at the least, a Twitter account, a Facebook fan page, and a blog.

Participate – There is no shortcut to becoming a member of a community and developing relationships on each social medium your company uses. Some simple ways to participate include sharing something, asking questions, answering questions, providing tips or hacks, and responding to the community.

Cross-promote – Once your company has published some content on each social media platform, it's a good idea to cross-promote each account or profile. For example, place a link to your company's Facebook fan page and Twitter account on the company website, place a link to the company blog on the company Twitter page, and import the company blog to the Facebook fan page. That way, when someone finds your company on one medium, they can also find it easily on the other mediums.

Leverage your assets – Your company always has more assets than it realizes. For example, if your company does not have time to create content, maybe it could instead repurpose content. If you have a blog, take one of the posts and turn it into 140 character tips that can be posted on Twitter. If you don't have a blog, maybe you have a book or new employee guides that can be repurposed. Maybe you have an employee whose job is to follow trends in the industry, who is consistently reading the latest links or news and could publish those on Twitter or create a blog post quickly. If you think creatively, you can always find something you already have and repurpose it for social media usage.

Case Study of Building a User Base: Alice

All of these tips are great for companies that already have some presence online or an established brand offline. But what if you haven't even officially launched your company yet? Even if you don't have a product yet, you can still start using social media!

Alice, a start-up company that uses a mail-order system to make sure you never run out of toilet paper and other home essentials, did just that for their June 2009 beta launch. To prepare, the company set up a Twitter account, blog, and Facebook fan page in January 2009. Alice cross-promoted each of these profiles and put up a placeholder website that had limited information about the service and links to the Twitter and Facebook profiles.

Alice built brand awareness on each of these mediums by offering quirky household tips, posting interesting and relevant links, and holding contests and giveaways related to consumer packaged goods that they already had, like shampoo and dog treats. Alice responded to questions and participated in conversations with moms and Gen Y professionals that were likely to use the service. The company even leveraged a simple asset – private beta invitations – by using its social media presence to find people across the United States to participate in a private beta launch and provide feedback to the company.

By the time Alice launched 6 months later, the company had an impressive 2000 Twitter followers, 500 Facebook fans, 200 blog posts, and numerous mentions and links from the blogging community.

This goes to show you the power of signing up early, participating in existing communities, cross-promoting, and leveraging any assets that you have. If Alice can do it without a product or a completed website, your company can too!

Component 2: Creating a remarkable message

There are two basic strategies for creating remarkable messages:

Having a remarkable company or product, and creating several little messages that add up over time

Latching on to another remarkable or compelling product in the form of doing a giveaway or contest to generate buzz

Truth be told, a good social media strategy incorporates both of these strategies to optimize budget, resources, and get the best results possible.

Several Little Messages that Add Up – Don't fall into the trap of needing that one big idea to create a viral campaign. In fact, creating several consistent and compelling messages over time can also add up to being generally remarkable, and generate just as much traffic and business and sales.

To figure out what makes your company remarkable, consider that most companies compete on one of these four attributes: time, price, quality, or variety. This is not to say a company can't be attractive on more than one of these dimensions, but the most successful companies stand out especially on one attribute alone.

For example, Alice competes on time. The concept is that you can automate your regular purchases and save time making lists of things you need or making unnecessary trips to the store. Likewise, a search engine called OneRiot also competes on time: it returns search results on the most newly-created content by scanning Twitter, Digg, and other social services, to deliver real-time, socially-driven results.

The point is that by looking at how your company competes, you can easily figure out what remarkable messages you want to broadcast. Though both these companies compete on time, each does it in its own way. Alice uses household hacks to engage its audience, while OneRiot uses a constant stream of (literally) up-to-the-minute news and "first look" updates. Both of these companies create compelling messages for their audiences: moms looking to save time in the household, and people obsessed with knowing the news first, respectively.

Here are some of the simplest compelling messages your company can create:

Links to interesting news, media, or content

Tips, tricks, or hacks

Questions, polls, or surveys

Collaborations between experts in a niche

Case Study of Creating Many Remarkable Messages: Careerealism

Careerealism is an online resource for men and women between the ages of 20 and 35 who are in need of career advice. The company's Twitter strategy utilizes many small but remarkable messages that add up over time to more followers, more sharing on Twitter, and ultimately, more traffic to the website.

Careerealism shares links from online newspapers, blogs, and other media outlets that are relevant to the company's audience: young professionals looking for jobs. Most of the links are related to career or employment. For every 5 links Careerealism tweets from other sources, it tweets 1 link from its own website. This helps Careerealism build credibility and come across as an expert source, rather than a feed full of self-promoting tweets.

Careerealism also interacts with readers and career experts by sponsoring the Twitter Advice Project, or T.A.P. How it works is Careerealism tweets a reader's question, then asks several career experts to tweet their answers. Careerealism retweets the answers using a tool called TweetBots so all of its readers can see. Careerealism also summarizes all the answers in a blog post, which is later posted on the website for subscribers.

Careerealism creates a lot of interesting content quickly using these tactics, and over time, has gained substantial traction. Careerealism has over 10,000 followers on Twitter and over 10,000 visitors per month to its website!

One Big Message: Giveaways and Contests – Still not sure how to turn your company's strategy or products into a remarkable message? No need to stress – you can always use a giveaway.

Giveaways are the ultimate way to create a compelling message in social media, especially when the items being given away are highly anticipated or highly valued.

Popular giveaway items at the moment include the iPhone (or anything that Apple makes), the Flip camera, plane tickets, donations to charity, or even cash. In general, goods valued at $200 or more, especially electronics, work well.

Example: Orbitz more than doubled its followers on Twitter by offering one free airline ticket to a lucky follower. In 6 hours, its follower count went from 2,600 to 5,600! If you want to calculate return on investment of a $500 plane ticket, Orbitz "paid" less than $0.17 per Twitter follower. That's much less than a banner ad would cost, and there's no telling how many more people Orbitz reached beyond the fractional 3,000 people that actually took action and followed them.

Case Study on the Power of Giveaways: I Will Teach You to Be Rich

Ramit Sethi recently launched a personal finance book called *I Will Teach You to Be Rich* onto the New York Times Bestseller list. Because the bestseller list is based on sales within a certain time period, part of Ramit's book launch strategy included a giveaway to anyone who purchased his book on or before its launch day and sent a copy of their receipt to Ramit via email. On the day his book came out, Ramit had a live streaming video where people could call in and ask him questions, and he answered them on air and via his Twitter account. During this live streaming video, Ramit did several giveaways, including prizes of $1000 and several Amazon Kindles. The money prize tied in well with his book because he billed it as "$1000 to jumpstart your personal finances." As a result of these prize giveaways,

Ramit was able to sell thousands of copies of his book, *I Will Teach You to Be Rich*, within just a few days of its release.

Component 3: Crafting a compelling reason to share

Finally, every viral marketing campaign gives people a compelling reason to share. That's where the name "viral marketing" comes from – the message becomes like a virus, where one person tells three people and the message multiplies and disperses. **Page 29 29** Social Media Marketing

Here are some key tips that will help your company give people a reason to share the message:

Use brand evangelists – Brand evangelists are people who are more fanatic than the average person would be about your brand or product. Apple is the classic example of a company that can build a cult-like user base. Your company may not be Apple, but if you have an email list or newsletter, let those people get your message first. It might be worthwhile to create a special email list for people who want to be in the know about your company.

Ask people to spread the message – Part of your company's message should be a gentle reminder to people to share it. If it is a giveaway, make sharing a part of the requirements to be eligible.If it is a poll or a contest, let people enter and get their friends to vote publicly on a social network like Twitter. Don't just expect people to share something, give them an incentive to share so that the message spreads.

Make sharing easy – For blog posts, you can make it easier to share something by placing buttons at the bottom of the post, such as "Share on Facebook" or "Vote on Digg." For Twitter, you can make sharing easier by keeping the message at around 120 characters, which allows people to retweet you without having to modify the message. No matter what the medium, it's important to make transferring information as effortless as possible.

Give sharing a push – If you are doing a big push and have a group of people who are willing to trade votes with you on social networking sites, feel free to ask for a vote during a certain time period. Don't use this option often though – only when you know the message is compelling. Some sharing sites, such as StumbleUpon, also have a way to purchase hits. If you notice a blog post doing well on StumbleUpon, you can help it along by paying $0.05 per targeted hit from its user base. If your message is compelling, those people will vote for your content and the extra push may help your company get to StumbleUpon's front page, which will send loads of traffic to your site.

Utilize existing resources – Take advantage of others' resources by integrating communication networks into your message. For example, posts that talk heavily about Twitter tend to do very well on Twitter; the same goes for every social network or bookmarking site. If you can incorporate the medium into your message, it is more likely to be shared.

Case Study of Leveraging Your Assets: Threadless

An interesting application of utilizing existing resources to create a compelling reason to share is what t-shirt company Threadless did when it launched the Twitter Tees section of its site. Threadless is an online retailer of t-shirts that lets its community vote on user-submitted designs (a concept called crowdsourcing). The designs that get the most votes end up getting printed by Threadless for retail.

So how did Threadless gain over 700,000 followers on Twitter and tons of publicity? It utilized its existing voting system and created a special section of its sitecalled Twitter Tees where people could submit funny tweets to be printed on t-shirts. The company already had the voting technology, already had the printing capacity, already had the online store, and already had a customer base. It used the resources it already had and created a compelling tie-in to a popular social networking service. It gave people a reason to share the message, because the only way to vote for a shirt is to tweet your vote. Finally, Threadless was able to secure some advertising in the top right corner of Twitter's network – advertising that is viewed by tens of millions of Twitter users every day.

Sales

This section talks specifically about using social media to build a sales pipeline that can be integrated into your company's current sales process. In this section, you'll find answers to questions like:

How do I drive traffic to my site?

How do I collect prospects information?

How do I turn prospects into leads?

Social media is a wonderful method for driving sales for your company. Using social media as part of your company's sales process is similar to any other method you might use. Use social media to generate prospects, and then capture prospects as leads. Finally, once you've captured your lead list, you can put those leads into your current sales process.

Find prospects

In social media, generating prospects usually means driving traffic to a website where you can collect lead information. There will be more information about collecting leads in the next section. In the viral marketing section, there was information about how to find your company's target audience. Naturally, finding prospects for your sales pipeline will be much easier the more you've connected with your audience on each of these platforms, in the form of subscribers, followers, fans, and friends. Now that you have an audience on several different social media platforms, here is how your company can drive traffic to a website with specific tools:

Blogs – One of the reasons every company should have a blog is because it adds text to the company website that attracts search engine traffic. Also, your blog can build a subscriber list of people who read the content regularly. Companies use blogs to have conversations with potential clients or customers and build credibility within the industry.

Some ways to optimize your company's blog include: promoting and republishing the content on all profiles, responding to each person's comment individually, making the RSS feed prominent (in the right hand corner) and putting links to all other social media profiles in front of the reader.

Facebook – Facebook has a wide array of options for companies, including, groups, fan pages, applications, and Facebook Connect.

To find clients on groups, start a group that is related to your company. If you have a company called Costumes „R Us that sells theatrical props, very few people will join a group called "Costumes „R Us." People will, however, join a group called "Sound of Music fans" or "I love Guys and Dolls." The nice thing about groups is that the administrator can send messages to the entire group, similar to an email list.

Facebook fan pages are similar to groups, except they are usually named after the company. With fan pages, your company can import blog posts, videos, and fans are able to leave messages on the wall. One special feature of fan pages is that people who are fans can recommend the fan page to their entire friend list at once. This is unlike almost every other Facebook feature, which only lets a user invite 20 of his or her friends per day.
When considering a Facebook app, remember that the types of applications that most Facebook users like are games or quizzes. The best app would be if you can turn

your product or service into a game with lots of levels, where there was incentive for players to recruit their friends to the game. If you were Costumes „R Us, a trivia quiz about musicals and theater productions where a player could challenge his friends would work well.

Twitter – The best way to find prospects on Twitter is to build that following! There are tips on how to do this in the viral marketing section of this book. Once you have a following, you can publish links to your website manually or by feeding your company's blog into Twitter using a service like TwitterFeed. This won't be true of everyone, but as a rule of thumb, Twitter users generally feel that 20% of self-promotion is the right amount. That means for every link to your company's site, post 4 links to other interesting resources.

StumbleUpon – If you want to get your article to do well on StumbleUpon there are a few ways to optimize it.

First, make sure you have a very strong title. Many StumbleUpon users don't read a post to the end, or they vote for it to remind themselves to read it in full later. The strongest of titles are the ones that indicate the post is a list. Lists with items in the 70's and 80's or higher do very well – in fact, the bigger the better when it comes to lists. The next thing is to make sure you optimize your company's website to have as little clutter as possible at the top so the post is the foremost thing on the page. Finally, add a stunning image near the top of the post, embedded in the text to make the post stand out.

Once the post is optimized, there is an option to send the post to friends on StumbleUpon and ask them to vote for it. If the post is doing well, you can give it a push to get it to StumbleUpon's front page by paying $0.05 per targeted hit.

Digg – Many of the same techniques for optimizing a StumbleUpon post also apply to Digg. One thing that's essential for Digg is putting a Digg button in the top right hand corner of the post, embedded in the words. Also, Digg's user base is very targeted and skews heavily towards twenty year old males, so unless your content appeals to that demographic, it probably won't do well.

A few other things to realize about Digg is that it is a user-driven site that has a small group of power users who control most of the content that hits the front page. If content is submitted by one of these power users, it is much more likely to get to the front page. Also, the Digg algorithm rewards content that gets lots of votes quickly – say within the first 30 minutes of submission. Finally, Digg allows people to talk about the submitted article on its site, and articles that have a conversation in the comments section tend to get more Diggs quickly.

Turning prospects to leads

Now that your company is able to drive traffic, how do you turn that traffic into a lead list? Two ways that work well are to create a membership portion of your company's site, or to build an email list.

Membership Section – Membership sections can be useful for creating a community around your company's products or services. The difficulty is that you have to give people a compelling reason to sign up, so this method may not be for everyone.

However, if you have a membership site already, Facebook Connect is a great tool for if your members match up with Facebook's demographics. In general, you'll lose a percentage of your audience any time people have to register to use your site; but with Facebook Connect, people can sign up for your site and import their Facebook information using their Facebook account. Many people, especially teens, remain logged into their Facebook accounts at all times. Facebook Connect also allows users to post their activity back to their Facebook accounts, creating a viral effect.

Google has a similar service that allows users to log in with their Gmail accounts. This does not quite have the same viral capabilities as Facebook with the sharing capabilities, but it does allow you to build membership profiles based on the user's Google information.

There is no rule that you have to use one or the other of these two services. You could use both Facebook and Google connect to offer members several options for logging in. The most important thing is that when you use one of these services, make sure your own website collects membership information so your company can develop its own lead list that's not dependent on Google or Facebook.

Email list – The second option for your company is to start building an email or newsletter list. Direct email marketing is still one of the most effective ways to get a response online. Most companies offer something for free – for example, a free **white paper, a** free Ebook, a free teleseminars, or free content in a newsletter – in exchange for contact information, such as name and email address.

With an email list, you can segment your users and track opens and clicks to suit your business needs. A newsletter also allows your company to plug its products or services on a regular basis, as long as you offer valuable information in addition to sales pitches.

Companies that use memberships and email lists to convert prospects to leads end up with more qualified leads to pass on to their sales team.

Turning leads into customers

At this point, your company has its lead list. Now, you can integrate this lead list with your current process and start reaping the benefits of using social media as part of your company's lead generation strategy.

Case Study on Finding B2B Leads: Brazen Careerist

Brazen Careerist is an online talent agency dedicated to providing tools to the HR departments of companies interested in recruiting Generation Y. The company put together a teleseminar and invited thousands of HR professionals to attend for free. Brazen Careerist found HR professionals by utilizing professional groups on LinkedIn and Facebook. Because the teleseminar was valuable to the incumbents, the offering gained even more traction with word-of-mouth and sharing via social media outlets.

In order to gain access to the seminar, each HR professional had to provide an email address and company contact information. Over 400 people signed up for the hour-long teleseminar. At the end of the seminar, Brazen Careerist asked professionals to submit any questions that hadn't been answered in the seminar.

Now, the company had a lead list of companies that were struggling with recruiting Generation Y, the name of someone within the organization and all the contact information necessary, plus a list of problems that HR professionals were trying to solve, regarding recruiting Generation Y. They gave this information to their sales department, who got to work on the phones. They also put out another informational packet to answer the most common questions HR professionals had, which built credibility and trust with the potential clients.

Customer Services

This section talks specifically about using to handle customer service issues. In this section, you'll find answers to questions like:

Why do customers want service support via social media?

Should my company have a separate account for customer service issues?

How can my company monitor and manage reputation with social media?

How does my companyhandle bad publicity on social media?

Building relationships with current customers is one of the most important things any company can do, but it's also one of the most neglected. Social media offers a solution to providing faster customer service to customers so companies can maintain their relationships and ensure repeat purchases.

Technical and Service Support

Most customers do not like calling a number when they have a problem with your products. In fact, customers expect that they will be put on hold, they will be ushered through a few customer service reps who will tell them their problem can't be solved to their liking, and then they will finally have to get angry and force the customer service reps to speak to someone who allows them to put in a special ticket that will take 7-10 days to be approved.

What a disaster for most companies.For a company that uses social media though, this could be a great opportunity to show your customers that customer service doesn't have to be this painful.

The truth is that most customers aren't angry about their original problem as long as it gets fixed quickly. In the end, customers are dissatisfied at the annoyance, wasted time, and extra hassle it takes to get their problem through customer services. Companies that allow customers to contact them via social media will be able to maintain relationships with their customers and have a high chance of that customer purchasing again.

One of the questions companies have about using social media for customer service is: Should we have a separate account for customer service on Twitter? This is up to the company and will probably be influenced by the company's size and the volume of support requests. The downsides are that people do not know how many accounts you have and will likely send support requests to whichever account they find first. Also, your company will be splitting its following between two or more accounts, which makes it difficult to grow each of the accounts to its full potential.

The benefit of using two accounts is you don't have to bore your followers with support answers. Some companies get around this by answering only the more unusual support requests publicly from their main account, and answering the general support requests via a direct message or via email.

Reputation Management

Customer service is just part of the bigger issue of reputation management. Two components of reputation management are monitoring your company's reputation so you can proactively respond to situations, and also so you can deal with any bad publicity your company or products may receive.

How to Monitor Your Company's Reputation

There are a few tools every company should use to monitor what people are saying.

Google Alerts – This is a Google service that sends you an alert based on the keywords you set up.

OneRiot or Twitter search– OneRiot is a real-time search engine that captures keywords on Twitter and social bookmarking sites. Search OneRiot for keywords about your company and respond to complaints or concerns about your product or service, or if your company is focused specifically on Twitter, Twitter has its own real-time search engine for just tweets.

Using these tools with the appropriate keywords will catch 99-100% of everything people are saying about your company, so you can respond appropriately and protect the brand.

Dealing with Bad Publicity

There are always situations where an experiment goes awry or someone just doesn't like your company, product, or service and wants to complain about it in a public forum. There are a few ways your company can deal with bad publicity on social media: calmly dispel it if the information is false, put a positive spin on it if the information is true, or ignore it if the information is purely opinion. Sometimes drawing attention to a dissenter is worse than allowing them to have and speak their opinions.

Here are some tips for responding to bad publicity:

Respond quickly to help control the message

Response should be short and to the point

Response should seem impromptu, but not unprofessional

Response must be warm, genuine, and authentic

Response must be in the right medium – don't use social media to respond to shareholders or mainstream media

It helps to have a relationship with your customer prior to the incident

Use the right person in your company to respond to the incident – your company's CEO is not always the best or most appropriate choice

Here are some tips specifically for the video medium:

Use Vimeo instead of YouTube for branding purposes

Memorize what you want to say and look directly at the camera

Don't let the ubiquity of the medium allow the video to look unprofessional – use good lighting, appropriate attire, and production makeup

Don't overproduce – professional videos look inauthentic

The shorter the better – viewers form impressions in the first 12 seconds

Don't become fodder for a junior comedian – people who know how to use video editing tools can remix the message to make fun of the entire video

Case Study on Reputation Management: Domino's Pizza

In March 2009, two Domino's Pizza employees released a YouTube video of themselves coughing and sneezing on a customer's food. Within one day the video had over 1 million hits on YouTube.

In Chicago, Domino's local operating partner, going by Twitter handle @dpzramon, tweeted reassurances about the cleanliness and employee training standards of his Chicago stores within hours of the video gaining publicity. He also sent individual messages to all of his Chicago friends on Twitter with the same information, and asked them to retweet the information to all of their followers.

A day later, Domino's CEO released a three minute response video via YouTube. He used strong language, calling what his employees did a felony, and saying he was sickened by their actions. He also was not looking at the camera directly, which made viewers question whether he was reading cue cards.

As you might be guessing, one of these approaches worked extremely well, and one of them didn't. Chicagoans who had received messages from @dpzramon came away with the feeling that the situation was handled appropriately and that their Domino's Pizza stores were well taken care of. In fact, Chicagoans wanted to buy pizza to support their friend @dpzramon.

The response to the Domino's CEO video was much different. People felt the video was too long, used too strong of language, did not seem genuine, and that the video seemed unprofessional. Viewers also criticized Domino's for not responding to the incident for several days, and for using the wrong media to put out a message that was more aimed at shareholders and the media than at Domino's Pizza customers.

Pillar 5: How to Measure Return on Investment

It's difficult to say how each company should quantitatively measure their social media efforts without knowing more about the company, but in general, anytime a company can convert metrics and analytics into dollars is usually the best approach. This is easier to do with sales and customer services usages, while more difficult to do with public relations, marketing, and research and development usages. Here are some metrics to keep in mind when trying to calculate the ROI of various services:

Email

Landing page conversion percentage

# of opens for each email

# of clicks of links in each email

# of email subscribers who purchase something

Blogs

Total # of posts or average page views per post

Traffic overall or per post via a service like Google Analytics

Subscriber counts via an RSS service like Feedburner

Comment counts per post (measures engagement)

Demographics information via a service like Quantcast

Facebook

of Fans of members in your group

Percentage of items shared on Facebook

Percentage of traffic driven to website

Facebook fan page analytics

Twitter

of followers

# of retweets of all links

# of people who respond (@) to questions, polls, etc.

Percentage of traffic driven to website

Became a trending topic or not

StumbleUpon

of reviews for submitted item

Traffic driven to site

Made it to the front page or not

# of people who subscribed or signed up after landing on the page

Digg

of Diggs

# of comments on the Digg site

Traffic driven to site

Made it to the front page or not

# of people who subscribed or signed up after landing on the page

Case study to calculate ROI: Naked Pizza

Naked Pizza is a New Orleans-based healthy pizza join that specializes in its low-calorie slices that weigh a fraction of a normal pizza slice. The company built a 4,300 person following on Twitter in 2.5 months. Though the company is local, Naked Pizza is still able to use Twitter to advertise within a 3 mile radius.

Using analytics tools to find entrance rates, Naked Pizza has found that, on average, 20% of sales come from users who enter the site via Twitter.

Furthermore, during one particular advertising blitz on Twitter, the company found that 69% of their sales for that day first came to the site via Twitter's website. The normal 20% of sales per day are sustained as long as CEO Jeff Leach tweets – which he does at least once and up to 15 times every single day.

Because Naked Pizza was able to change their analytics metrics into dollars, the company was able to make an important business decision: to change their company sign, which originally had an order phone number on it, to their Twitter handle. By the way, Naked Pizza gets an average of 35,000 people who drive by every day, and is working to become a national chain.